To Helen & Graham; my mom and dad. For believing in me and allowing me to follow my dream.

Published by Morse-Brown Publishing and How2hats
Series Editor: John Morse-Brown
Step-by-step photography © John Morse-Brown
Model photography © Talia White taliawhitephotography.com
Model: Madeline Scriven
Model make-up: Kari Roberts
Design © Morse-Brown Design Ltd. morsebrowndesign.co.uk
For more titles in this series, see www.how2hats.com

ISBN: 9781907615184

CONTENTS

Great Aunt Millie, middle,
in her dapper suit!

INTRODUCTION

Flowers have adorned hats for centuries, fresh or hand-made, and there's no doubt that they add a marvellous flourish of colour and life to any headpiece. The flowers I've chosen for this book are the flowers I make most often in my day-to-day work. By learning how to make them yourself, you'll be able to transform any hat or headpiece into a work of art.

All of this started for me with a love of textiles, a passion for sculpture and an MA course, after which I set up Sharper Millinery. Coming from a creative background, I was always encouraged to try new techniques and to follow my dreams by very supportive parents, but I really have to thank my very stylish Great Aunt Millie (opposite) for introducing me to millinery.

I create hats for weddings, the races and special events, and I often use silk flowers as a way of matching the colours in a client's outfit to their hat or headpiece. Many of my hats have won awards at Racing ladies days for being the best hat or complimenting the outfit for the best-dressed lady. I launch a summer and winter collection each year as I develop new techniques and styles for brides and racing ladies.

For me, millinery is artwork for your head – something totally unique. Wearing a one-off, handmade headpiece gives the wearer confidence, poise and elegance that nothing else can quite match.

Sally.

Chapter 1

PREPARATION

As is often said, preparation is everything. In this chapter I will talk you through all the things you'll need in order to venture into the wonderful world of flower making.

TOOLS & EQUIPMENT

It's always nice to find a skill or hobby that doesn't require a vast outlay on new tools and equipment. Having said that, in a funny kind of way, I actually like having to purchase new tools, as long as they're not going to completely break the bank. Choosing the tools, waiting for them to arrive in the post, handling them for the first time – it's such a pleasure.

The full set of flower making tools, from **Guy Morse-Brown Hat blocks:** www.hatblocks.co.uk

Happily, the art of silk flower making fulfils both of these criteria. Most of the tools you'll need you will find lying around the house already, but the one set of special tools that you require are not actually very expensive at all, and they're extremely nice to own and handle...

You will need:

- **Flower making Tools** (see opposite).
  Stainless steel or brass tools are best for flower making. If they are steel, make sure they are *stainless* steel, as plain steel tools will rust. Stainless steel also has better heat retention than brass, so you can work them longer. You can buy electric tools or manual tools – for this book we are using manual tools, with a portable electric hot plate.

- **A portable electric hotplate** (see opposite).
  I purchased mine from Amazon.

- **A sponge/piece of foam and a smooth tea towel or piece of cotton or calico** (not a synthetic fabric as this will burn. See photo on page 22). Wrap the sponge or piece of foam in the tea towel or cotton/calico sheet (one you don't mind getting burnt). This is where you will work with your flower making tools.

- **Dye or paint** (see pages 12–15).

- **A pair of sharp fabric scissors**

- **A pair of blunt-nose scissors**

- **UHU or multi-purpose glue**

- **A roll of floristry wire**

- **Cotton wool balls**

- **Stamens/beads/crystals/pompoms**
  All optional – see the individual chapters for more details on these.

More on the tools

There are many types of flower making tools, and many different shapes and sizes. Each shape and size has a specific job. You can either purchase the full set as shown opposite (www.hatblocks.co.uk), or you can just buy the ones you'll need for this book. These are as follows:

- 20mm ball for the quick rose, peony and anemone

- 30mm ball for traditional rose, poppy and peony

- Rat tail/hook tool for traditional rose and quick rose

- Knife tool for the poppy and anemone

FABRICS

As well as being able to purchase a set of shiny new tools, you're going to be working with some of the most beautiful fabrics in the world, and one of the most ancient.

Silk is such a gorgeous fabric to work with and to wear. Say the word 'silk' and people think 'luxury' and 'elegance'. It has been used by the Chinese for centuries, and the Romans valued it similarly to gold. It both dyes well and retains it's shape – both essential characteristics for flower making.

Having said all this, you can actually use any natural materials with the instructions in this book. But do make absolutely sure that the fabric you are going to use is natural (i.e. not synthetic). If there are any synthetic fibres present in the fabric they will melt with the heat of the flower making tools. And you'll end up with a very nasty mess (and smell!).

In this book we use three different types of silk: silk dupion, silk organza and silk habotai.

SILK DUPION

One of the most popular silks in the world –
it's unique beauty comes from the 'slubs' or
imperfections in the fabric which run through it.
The type we are using is also known as a 'shot'
fabric, which means that it is woven with the warp
and weft in two different colours (red and white
in this case), which make it shimmer, and which
give it it's pink colour. It's a bit like *pointillism* –
the technique of painting in small, discreet, dots
of colour, which the eye then merges to make a
different colour.

Note: When you stiffen silk dupion, the colour
changes slightly. This is because the stiffening
process bonds the fibres together more closely. This
is very important if you are trying to match a flower
to the material in someone's outfit...

Silk dupion: Top: unstiffened, bottom: stiffened.

SILK ORGANZA (OR ORGANDIE)

This is a lightweight yet stiff type of silk, perfect for
'papery' petals or leaves. We use it in this book for
the poppy on page 47.

SILK HABOTAI

This is another lightweight silk fabric that is great
for creating vintage-style flowers. We use it for the
narcissus on page 39.

STIFFENING THE FABRIC

There are several reasons why you need to stiffen the fabric. Firstly, cut silk frays very easily, and stiffening stops the fraying and makes the flowers look more crisp. Secondly, it allows the petals to retain the shapes you give them with the flower tools. Without stiffening, the petals would very quickly flatten out.

There are specialist fabric stiffeners out there, which you can of course use, but I prefer to use standard PVA/Elmer's glue that you can purchase from any hardware or craft store, or even budget stores in small bottles. In my experience, it's as good as the expensive alternatives, if not better.

You'll need a brush, some plastic sheeting with which to line your working area (a cut-open plastic carrier bag works just as well), and  a pot in which to mix your stiffener. I find plastic take-away cartons work a treat – preferably with a lid. You can then keep the mixture for next time.

1 Mix the PVA and water in the ratio of one part PVA to 5 parts water (1:5 PVA:water). It should have the consistency of yoghurt.

2 Starting from the top, brush away from you, working down the fabric towards you, so you don't end up dipping your clothes in the glue.

4 When the fabric is completely covered, hang it up to dry. An outside line on a sunny day is best, (10 – 15 minutes), otherwise inside is fine. It will drip as it's drying, so protect your floor with newspaper. Even if you are using the washing line outside, I tend to still use a coat-hanger, so I don't get glue all over my washing line.

PAINTING THE FABRIC

There are many ways to add colour to or change the colour of fabrics. You can use dye baths, dip dye them, or paint them. I prefer to paint my fabric. You can choose to paint all of your petals individually before you cut them out, but I prefer to paint the whole sheet of fabric in one go. That way I feel you get a more natural look to your flowers, and every petal doesn't look the same, much like nature.

I use silk paints to paint my fabric. Silk paints contain a fixative, making the painting and fixing a one-step process. (If you choose to use dyes you will also need salt to fix the colour, and the colour can still end up running if the fabric gets wet.) I also like the way silk paints can be used like watercolour paints, creating a wash of different colours, giving a more interesting effect to your petals and leaves.

I've tried lots of methods over the years, and this is the one that I've discovered works best for me. Feel free to experiment with other methods, but this is the one I'm going to show you now.

I tend to paint about half a meter (1 ½ feet) of fabric at a time, but this does depend on the space you have available. I usually cover my working surface with a plastic sheet, making it easy to transfer your wet fabric to your drying place. I also often do it outside on a sunny or breezy day. But you can do it inside, as I have shown here.

1. Spread out your plastic sheet on your table or workbench, and make sure you have the paint, a bowl of water, your brushes and some kitchen towel to hand.

If you were going to dip dye the fabric, you'd need to dye it first, and then stiffen it, but with painting, it is the other way round – we stiffen it first and then paint it. So we start with a sheet of stiffened fabric. In the steps below, I'm painting the fabric for the poppy (see pg 47), with two colours. The colours blend nicely into each other, giving a lovely mottled effect.

2. Start by brushing the paint on. I find a bigger brush is better than a smaller one, as you can cover more fabric quickly.

3 Now start to merge the colours. Like watercolours, the paints wash into each other beautifully. Flick water on to help with the merging.

5 Lift the painted fabric off the plastic sheet and hang it up to dry. Pegging it on to a coat hanger I find is the easiest method.

4 Carry on until the fabric is covered, although there's no need to paint right up to the edges of the fabric.

6 In the spirit of 'waste not, want not' you can soak up the left-over paint with a fresh piece of silk, and create more coloured fabric at the same time.

7 When it's nice and dry you're ready to start making your flowers.

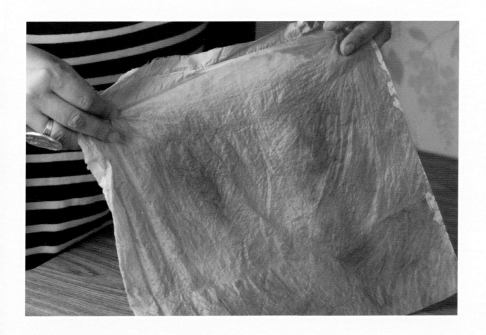

Chapter 2

TRADITIONAL ROSE

In this chapter I'm going to show you how to create a traditional rose using individually cut petals. The chapter following this one demonstrates a faster and easier method that I have developed for making roses, that produces almost identical results. Both methods use the same fabric and painted effects, but I wanted to first show you how to make a rose the traditional way, so that you can decide which method works best for you (and so that you have the quick method up your sleeve if you're ever pushed for time on a big job...)

THE TRADITIONAL ROSE

First decide what colour and texture you'd like your rose to have. Silk organdie works extremely well for roses used in multiples on a hat, or if you're looking for a vintage-styled rose, silk dupion works well.

Prepare your chosen fabric according to the instructions on pages 10–15, cut out the templates on page 70, and then follow these simple steps to create your perfect traditional rose.

YOU WILL NEED:

- A piece of stiffened silk dupion, approximately 90 x 50cm (35 x 20 inches), or ½ metre (20 inches) of 36 inch wide fabric if you are purchasing it specifically for this project. See instructions on pages 10–15 for fabric preparation
- A portable electric hotplate
- A sponge or piece of foam and smooth tea towel
- Cotton balls or a wad of cotton wool
- A length of floristry wire – 50cm (20") will do
- A roll of floristry tape
- A 30mm ball flower making tool
- A rat tail/hook flower making tool
- A pair of blunt-nose scissors
- UHU or multi-purpose glue
- A biro

 3–4 hours, spread over a day to allow for drying time.

 Intermediate

STAGE 1: CREATING THE PETALS

 Photocopy and cut out your petals from the templates on page 70. Place the templates so that the bias of the fabric runs at a diagonal along the fabric. Draw around the set amount of petals in each size on the fabric. I use a biro rather than a pencil, and cut inside the line, as pencils tend to smudge.

 Carefully cut out each petal, making sure there are no marks at the edges of the petals. As you can see, I'm using children's scissors – I find these are better than proper dress-making scissors as their rounded noses are less likely to catch in the silk fibres.

 Lay your petals in piles according to their size. Switch on your electric ring and place the ball and hook tool on it, on a medium setting, to heat up.

Put your sponge and tea towel in front of you ready to work on.

IMPORTANT Before using your tools on the silk, test both the ball and the hook on the tea towel. If you create burn marks on the tea towel, the tools are too hot. Allow them to cool and turn the ring down.

 Starting with a small petal, and holding the pointed edge, push the heated ball tool into the surface of the petal as shown, below left. This should create a 'cup' effect in the petal. Repeat this on all of the petals – every size. The photo bottom right shows you what each petal should look like afterwards.

5 Now turn the petals over so that the cup is facing upwards and the pointed edge of the petal is facing away from you.

Hold the pointed edge between your fingers, and starting from one side of the petal, about 5mm (¼ inch) in from the edge, run the hook tool around to the bottom of the petal (the opposite end to the pointed end), creating a fold on one side of the petal. Repeat this on the opposite side of the petal. The photo at the bottom of the page shows you how the petal should look when you're finished.

6 Repeat this for all of the remaining petals. When you've done them all, it's advisable to again stack them in order of size – it just makes it easier to assemble the rose.

7 Turn off the electric ring and allow the tools to cool down.

STAGE 2: CREATING THE ROSE

1 You can make an 'open' rose or a 'closed' rose – i.e. one with the bud open or closed. I'm showing you how to make a closed rose.

Take your piece of cotton wool and your length of millinery wire, and wrap the wire centrally around the piece of cotton wool.

2 Now fold the top third of the cotton wool down over the wire, and the bottom third up, and then wrap the wire around the (now smaller) cotton wool pad again.

3 Twist the wires neatly together to create a longish stem for your rose. It's worth having a long stem as you will need it later to pull on.

4　We're now going to start glueing the petals on. Get your glue ready – take the first of the bud petals (one of the five), and place a small blob of glue on the petal on the inside of the cup. Stick this petal around the cotton wool ball. The bent-over lip of the petal should be facing out from the centre.

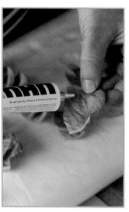 

5　Glue and add the next bud petal, on the opposite side of the cotton wool, making sure it overlaps the first petal as shown.

6　Turn the rose through ninety degrees and add the next two petals, each overlapping the other as before. Place each petal a little higher up the rose as shown in the photo below right.

Don't be afraid to squeeze the central petals – if you look at a real rose, you'll see the petals in the middle look quite crushed – that's the look we're aiming for.

7　Keep adding the remaining petals, in size order from smallest to largest, with each petal overlapping the other. Soon, it should start to look something like the photo opposite.

8 As the flower gets bigger, I find it easiest to work with it upside down. It gives you better access to the petals, and you can see what you are doing more easily.

9 Keeping building the flower up, turning it and overlapping the petals as you go. Keep washing your fingers too, so you don't get the rose messy with strands of glue.

After each layer of petals has been added, place the flower between your index and middle fingers and pull firmly down on the wire. This will ensure the petals are all firmly attached. (And this is where you benefit from having a reasonably long piece of wire, as it gives you something to grip on).

10 Keeping going until you have added all of the petals. Give the rose a final pull and hang it up by the wire stem for the glue to dry – about 30 minutes to one hour should be sufficient.

11 Depending on how you are going to use your rose, you may want to tidy up the back. The easiest way to do this is with floristry tape – a really clever, non-sticky tape that magically becomes sticky when you stretch it.

IDEAS TO STEAL

Six black roses were used to create this dramatic headpiece in velvet and organza. They were stitched onto a wide headband and finished with millinery net.

A coffee-bean, felt headpiece, adorned with a single silk dupion chocolate rose and finished with long stripped coq feathers. A very simple headpiece that can be worn at the front or side of the head.

Chapter 3

QUICK ROSE

This is a method I have developed for when I need to produce more than one rose at a time, or for when time is short. I always offer my customers the choice between a traditional rose and the quick rose, but most of the time they can't tell the difference between the two methods anyway, especially if they are placed in a bunch or overlaid.

THE QUICK ROSE

As with the traditional rose, first decide what colour and texture you'd like, and what fabric will work best for you. The quick rose demonstrated here is made from dyed silk dupion. For a more delicate flower, silk organdie works really well.

Prepare your fabric according to the instructions on pages 10–15, cut out the template on page 71, and follow these simple steps to create your perfect quick rose.

YOU WILL NEED:

- A piece of stiffened silk dupion, approximately 90 x 50cm (35 x 20 inches), or ½ metre (20 inches) of 36 inch wide fabric if you are purchasing it specifically for this project. See the instructions on pages 10–15 for fabric preparation
- A portable electric hotplate
- A sponge or piece of foam and smooth tea towel
- A 20mm ball flower making tool
- A rat tail/hook flower making tool
- A pair of blunt-nose scissors
- A biro

 1–2 hours, spread over a day to allow for drying time.

 Easy

Note This is one of those projects where it is a good idea to read though all of the steps before you begin.

1 Take the silk and measure a strip approximately 7cm (2 ¾ inches) wide by 50cm (20 inches) long, across the grain, to fit the height of your template.

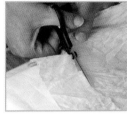

2 Place the template at one end of the strip and fold the strip under itself, to the exact width of the template, and keep folding, back and forth, until the whole strip has been concertinaed up as shown below.

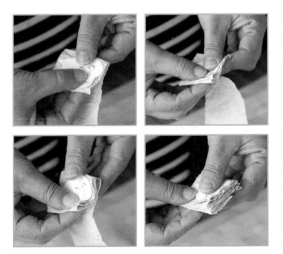

3 Place your petal template on top of the concertinaed strip, making sure the sides line up with the edges of the folds (this is very important). If they don't, re-fold your strip so that they do.

Draw around your template and then cut through the concertinaed fabric, *except* for a small section on each side of the template – just as you would if you were making one of those line of joined-up paper people. What you're aiming for is a line of petals, all joined together at the sides. If you cut *all* around the petal instead of leaving little uncut sections on each side, you will get lots of separate petals instead of the joined up line of petals that we're looking for.

31

4 Here's what the strip of petals should look like if you've done it correctly.

5 Now use the ball and the hook tools to create the same shapes, as you did with the traditional rose on pages 21 and 22. Start with the ball tool and finish with the hook tool.

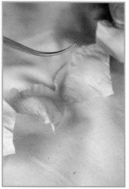

6 Next, start to roll the line of petals up, securing the roll with simple tacking stitches as you go along.

7 For a larger rose, just make one or two more strips of petals, based on the medium and large petal templates. Add these strips around the small rose, and stitch as you fold them around. You might need to use a thimble as the base of the rose becomes thicker.

8 And here is the finished rose. Both roses in the photo below are created from hand-painted silk dupion to give a varied colour tone, as you would see on a real rose. This means that every one of your flowers will be completely unique. The top flower is created with two 7cm (2 ¾ inches) strips and the bottom flower with only one.

IDEAS TO STEAL

An ivory, silk dupion rose, half circlet bridal piece. This is a very simple way of using the rose and giving it a lovely vintage feel.

I created smaller flowers for the other side of the head, just by using a smaller petal template.

ANOTHER IDEA TO STEAL

This rose has been created in the same way as the rose in this chapter, but it doesn't have the petal shapes cut into it, giving it it's delicate, gossamer look. Attached to an ivory, hand-blocked parasisal cloche.

Chapter 4
NARCISSUS

You can make these gorgeous, delicate little flowers in a whole range of shapes, sizes and colours, but for this project, I have chosen white petals with an orange trumpet. Perfect for a vintage headband.

NARCISSUS

You can make these lovely little beauties from left-over silk that you may have collected from creating other flowers. That's exactly what I've done here, using some white silk habotai and a piece of orange painted silk organdie from my poppy project (see page 47).

Prepare your chosen fabric according to the instructions on pages 10–15, cut out the templates on page 71, and then follow these simple steps to create a gorgeous narcissus (or six).

YOU WILL NEED:

- A small piece of stiffened white silk habotai for the petals, approximately 8 x 16cm (3 x 6 inches) square. And a small piece of painted, stiffened silk organdie for the centre, approximately 8x 4cm (3 x 1½ inches). See the instructions on pages 10–15 for fabric preparation.
- A portable electric hotplate
- A sponge or piece of foam and smooth tea towel
- A knife blade flower making tool
- A pair of sharp scissors
- Seed beads (I have used gold)
- Needle and ivory thread
- A biro

 1 hour

 Easy – intermediate

1 Draw around the templates (page 71) onto your chosen fabrics and cut them out.

2 Heat the knife blade tool and have your sponge and tea towel ready. Run the knife blade tool along the centre of each petal, starting at the centre of the star shape. Repeat for the other star shape.

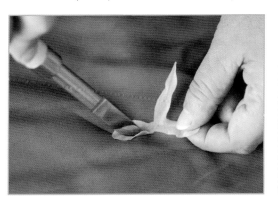

3 Now take the rectangular trumpet piece of painted silk, and make marks across the width of it with the knife tool, until it begins to curl round on itself.

4 Now to construct the flower. Take the two star-shaped pieces and lay them on top of each other so that the petals are offset. Stitch them together in the centre with a few tacking stitches.

5 Take the curled trumpet piece and fold one third of the width over onto itself. Roll it up lengthwise into a tube shape, so that the folded-up third is on the inside of the roll. Overlap the ends slightly and sew them together with a tacking stitch.

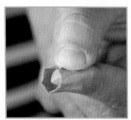 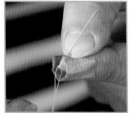

6 Place the trumpet in the centre of the petals, and using very small stitches, stitch it to the petals. This can be quite fiddly but it'll come with practice. Don't cut the thread – you'll use it next to attach the beads.

7 I've used tiny gold beads to finish my flower. Thread four or five beads onto your cotton and sew the free end back through the centre of the flower. Repeat this next to the first set of beads, as shown in the lower photo. If there is still space, and you feel it needs more beads, repeat the process in the centre.

8 And here's the finished narcissus. Very simple and very effective, especially in multiples.

IDEAS TO STEAL

I use droplets on many of my headpieces to give a vintage feel – on this headpiece I've used rose gold chain. You could use crystals, pearls or diamantes.

This beautiful bridal cluster demonstrates how you can combine several of the flowers in this book to create a really lovely vintage bouquet. The narcissus petals are used on this piece in ivory and pale pink, with pearls and diamantes.

Chapter 5

POPPY

This is one of my favourite flowers, with its bold, colourful petals. I love having a selection of different poppies in my garden as a reference when making silk poppies. This orange poppy is inspired by a meadow flower and adds a dynamic finish to any hat or headpiece. The flower can also be made as a brooch or a pin, adding a beautiful flourish of colour to a suit or jacket.

POPPY

This poppy is based on a wild poppy that tends to be smaller and more delicate than your standard poppy. I painted the silk using a mix of orange and deep red to give a varied colour throughout the petals, as this is what I'd observed from the poppies I'd found. And the 'paper' quality of the stiffened silk works perfectly here.

Prepare your chosen fabric according to the instructions on pages 10–15, cut out the template on page 71, and then follow these simple steps to create a perfect poppy.

- A piece of stiffened and painted silk organdie or silk habotai for the petals, approximately 40 x 7cm (16 x 3 inches). See the instructions on pages 10–15 for fabric preparation.
- A portable electric hotplate
- A sponge or piece of foam and smooth tea towel
- A 30mm ball flower making tool
- A knife blade flower making tool
- A pair of blunt-nosed scissors
- A box of pins
- A small black pompom
- Needle and black thread
- Seed beads of your choice
- A biro

 1 hour, spread over a couple of hours to allow for drying time.

 Easy

1 Draw round the template (page 71) onto your chosen fabrics, six times, and cut them out with your blunt-nosed scissors. As I've mentioned before, I tend to use a biro rather than a pencil (as pencil lines tend to smudge) and then make sure I cut the petal out *inside* the biro lines so no marks show on the silk.

2 Heat the ball and knife blade tools, with your sponge and cloth ready. Push the ball tool into the centre of each petal, while holding the pointed end.

 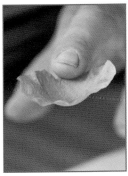

3 Using the heated knife blade tool, crinkle the outer edge of each petal as shown below.

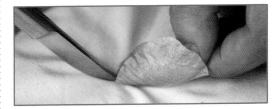

4 Take three of the petals and lay them over each other, with the points together, overlapping so they make a semi-circular shape as shown. Pin into place, and repeat with the remaining three petals.

5 Here's how both sets should now look.

6 Stitch each set of petals together with a few tacking stitches, so that the pointed ends are joined.

7 Stitch the two sets of petals to each other with small tacking stitches, making sure they are evenly placed. You may want to pin them together before you stitch, or if you're feeling confident, just hold them together while you stitch.

8 Take a black pompom and place it into the centre of the flower. Stitch into place, making sure you go through the pompom and petals a few times to hold it securely in place.

I've added a few seed beads around the pompoms. Add whatever works best with your choice of materials.

I love combining different
materials with contrasting colours
to create striking headpieces.
It really makes them stand out.

IDEAS TO STEAL

These poppies were made with
much larger petals and have
beaded centres.

Chapter 6

PEONY

I adore this flower – it's a sure sign that summer is on its way!
I have chosen to re-create it using a vivid pink silk dupion,
giving it it's beautiful array of bright pink shades. Peonies are
perfect to make into hair pins, to embellish headpieces, or as
bunches of flowers for a table centre-piece or bouquet. They
are very versatile flowers.

PEONY

This beautiful cluster flower can be created with hand-dyed silk dupion or with bought coloured silk. Hand-dyed silk dupion will give you beautiful tones and shades within the petals. You can also add extra sets of petals to give your flower a fuller appearance.

The centre of each flower can be created using small stamens or clusters of crystals or beads.

Prepare your chosen fabric according to the instructions on pages 10–15, cut out the templates on page 72, and then follow these simple steps to create a beautiful peony.

YOU WILL NEED:

- A piece of stiffened and painted silk dupion or silk organdie for the petals, approximately 40 x 7cm (16 x 3 inches). See the instructions on pages 10–15 for fabric preparation.
- A portable electric hotplate
- A sponge or piece of foam and smooth tea towel
- A 20mm ball flower making tool
- A 30mm ball flower making tool
- A pair of blunt-nosed scissors
- A length of floristry wire – 50cm (20") will do
- UHU or multi-purpose glue
- A bunch of stamens of your choice
- A biro

 2–3 hours, spread over a day to allow for drying time.

 Intermediate – difficult

1 Draw round the templates (see page 72) onto your chosen fabrics, in biro, and cut them out with your blunt-nosed scissors. If you want to make a bigger flower, cut out five more of each size petal.

2 Heat the ball tools and have your cloth and foam ready. First take one of the daisy-shaped centre pieces and push the 20mm ball tool into the centre of each of the small petals, and also into the centre of the daisy shape itself. Repeat for the other three centre pieces.

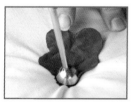

3 Now take the other petals and push the 30mm ball tool into the centre of each as shown in the photo opposite.

4 Keep going until you have done this to all of the petals. Then place them in piles according to size – it just makes it easier when you come to put the flower together.

5 Now to choose your stamens. I've gone for the white ones with pink heads, mirroring the colour of the silk. But there are lots of different styles available.

6 Twist a bunch of the stamens together with the floristry wire. Now bend them so all the heads face outwards, and bend the wire around the base of the stamens to keep them all together. Twist the wires neatly together to create a long stem for the peony.

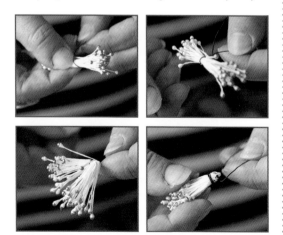

7 Take the four daisy-shaped petals and fold each in half. Make a small cut in the centre of each piece.

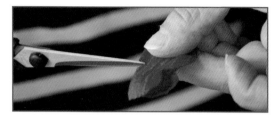

8 Thread the stamens through the hole of the first daisy-shaped petal as shown.

9 Push the stamens through the cuts in each of the other three daisy shaped pieces, adding a spot of glue in the centre of each piece until they have all been added. As you add each one, turn it a bit in relation to the one above, so you can see all of the petals.

10 Starting with the small petals, add a little blob of glue to the pointed base of each and press it on to the back of the flower. Each petal should overlap the previous petal slightly. Keep turning the flower as you add petals.

11 Repeat with the medium and large petals until they have all been glued to the flower. Now place the wire stem between your first and second fingers and pull on the flower to push the petals together and make sure they are all firmly attached.

12 Hang the flower upside down to dry. (I attach it to a coat hanger). This will ensure the petals don't get crushed as the glue dries – about 30 minutes to one hour should be ample.

IDEAS TO STEAL

A combination of white and pink peonies created in different sizes, with feather and crin trims.

A selection of roses, peonies and dahlias add a glorious finishing touch to this wide-brimmed sinamay hat.

Chapter 7

ANEMONE

This flower has very simple petals but is known more for its spikey, black centre. I have made these in many different pastel and bright colours, and it's the one flower to which I sometimes like to add leaves for a nice colour contrast.

ANEMONE

I find that silk dupion is best for anemones as it gives the closest likeness to the natural flower. I have used fringing for the centre, but you could use wire, single threads or beads to produce a similar effect.

Prepare your chosen fabric according to the instructions on pages 10–15, cut out the templates on page 71, and then follow these simple steps to create a beautiful peony.

YOU WILL NEED:

- A piece of stiffened silk dupion for the petals, approximately 40 x 7cm (16 x 3 inches). See the instructions on pages 10–15 for fabric preparation.
- A portable electric hotplate
- A sponge or piece of foam and smooth tea towel
- A 20mm ball flower making tool
- A knife blade flower making tool
- A pair of blunt-nosed scissors
- A small black pompom
- A length of black fringing
- Needle and black thread
- A biro

 1 hour

 Easy

1 Draw round the anemone templates (see page 71) onto your chosen fabrics, in biro, and cut them out. As you can see I'm also making leaves – they don't feature on the headpiece shown at the beginning of this chapter but I wanted to show you how to make them anyway.

2 Heat your ball and knife flower making tools and have your sponge and cloth ready. Push the ball tool into the centre of each petal in turn, and into the centre of the shape, just as you did for the peony on page 57. Repeat for the other piece.

3 Use the knife flower making tool to create vein markings along the centre of each of the leaves, as shown below.

4 Overlap the two daisy-shaped pieces so that the petals are offset from each other, and stitch them together through the centre with a few tacking stitches.

5 Cut a piece of fringing, approximately 5cm (2 inches) long and stitch with a running stitch along its length. Pull on the thread to gather the fringing into a circle. This will form the centre of your anemone.

6 Stitch the fringing into the centre of the petals with a few tacking stitches sewn right through the flower.

7 Finally, sew the pompom into the centre of the fringing, and the leaves on to the back.

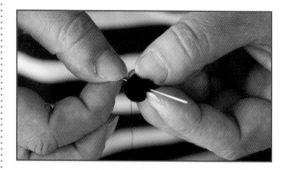

Opposite: A close-up view of the finished anemones (without the leaves in this case).

IDEAS TO STEAL

I often use contrasting colours in my work to make the flowers really stand out. This works well here, with the bright yellow anemones and the cobalt blue bubble crin headpiece. The centres were made using black wire to create the spikes.

The small pink flowers on this headpiece were created with the anemone template and small stamens rather than fringing.

TEMPLATES

These templates are displayed at their
correct size – just photocopy the pages.

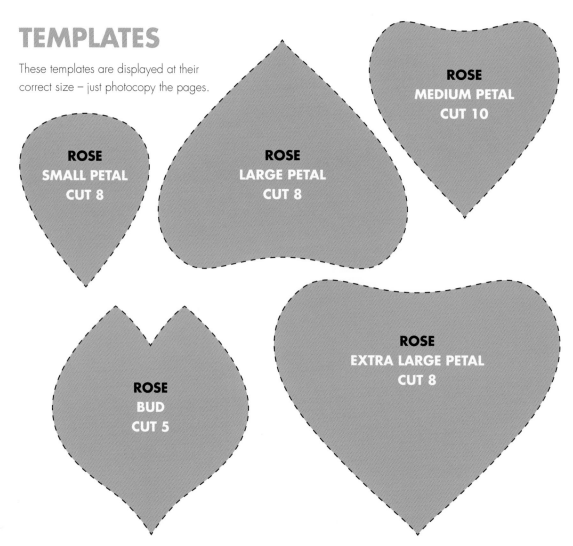

ROSE
SMALL PETAL
CUT 8

ROSE
LARGE PETAL
CUT 8

ROSE
MEDIUM PETAL
CUT 10

ROSE
BUD
CUT 5

ROSE
EXTRA LARGE PETAL
CUT 8

QUICK ROSE

ANEMONE
CUT 2

NARCISSUS
CUT 2

POPPY
CUT 6

ANEMONE
LEAF: CUT 2–5

NARCISSUS
CUT 1

PEONY
CENTRE
CUT 4

PEONY
EXTRA LARGE PETAL
CUT 8

PEONY
MEDIUM PETAL
CUT 10

PEONY
LARGE PETAL
CUT 8

PEONY
SMALL PETAL
CUT 8

72

SUPPLIERS

UK
Fabrics
Fancy Silk Store: 25 Moat Lane, B5 5BD Birmingham   **www.fancysilkstore.co.uk**

James Hare Silks   **www.james-hare.com**

General materials
MacCulloch & Wallis: 25-26 Dering Street, London W1S 1AT   **www.macculloch-wallis.co.uk**

Parkin Fabrics: Unit E Prince of Wales Business Park, Oldham OL1 4ER   **www.parkinfabrics.co.uk**

Hat Blocks
Guy Morse-Brown Hat Blocks   **www.hatblocks.co.uk**

IRELAND
Fabrics
Roisin Cross Silks   **www.silks.ie**

EUROPE
General materials
De Vroey Hats   **www.devroeyhats.be**

USA
Hats by Leko   **www.hatsupply.com**

Silk U Need   **www.silkuneed.com**

Judith M Inc: Tel: 1 (260) 499 4407   **www.judithm.com**

AUSTRALIA
Torb & Reiner: 101 Poath Road, Murrumbeena 3163, Victoria, Australia   **www.torbandreiner.com**

Silk Trader: 639 Burwood Rd, Hawthorn East, VIC 3123 Australia   **www.silktrader.com.au**

AND LOTS MORE HAT & FASCINATOR MAKING BOOKS...   **www.how2hats.com**

A BIG THANK YOU

Without the help and patience from many people, this book would not have happened...

To How2hats for approaching me to write the book in the first place – something I have thought about doing for a long time, but never imagined I would ever get around to doing.

Very importantly, to Kenny, my lovely husband, who encourages me in everything I do; who fuels new ideas and puts up with materials slowly filling every room. And the odd pin on the floor.

Also to Nicola at Parkin Fabrics who refuelled my passion for creating silk flowers, and to Deb, Racquel and Annette who visit my 'hat sweetie shop' on a regular basis and wear my work so well.

And of course to a great team that make my work really shout out. The very talented photographer Talia White, who has an exceptional eye for capturing my hats; make-up artists Kari Roberts and Preeti Bains for interpreting my ideas, and to models Madeline Scriven, Hannah Gardner, Rebecca Fisher, Caron Garland and Emma Jane Pick for always looking fabulous in whatever I ask them to wear.

Finally, to everyone who has purchased this book – thank you so much. It means a great deal to me. I hope you enjoy it and develop a new passion as I have done.